FEEL THE BEAT

R&B MUSIC

Tricia Hoffman

Gareth Stevens
PUBLISHING

Please visit our website, www.garethstevens.com. For a free color catalog of all our high-quality books, call toll free 1-800-542-2595 or fax 1-877-542-2596

Cataloging-in-Publication Data

Names: Hoffman, Tricia.
Title: R&B music / Tricia Hoffman.
Description: Buffalo, NY : Gareth Stevens Publishing, 2027. | Series: Feel the beat | Includes glossary and index.
Identifiers: ISBN 9781482480665 (pbk.) | ISBN 9781482480672 (library bound) | ISBN 9781482480689 (ebook)
Subjects: LCSH: Rhythm and blues music--History and criticism--Juvenile literature.
Classification: LCC ML3521.H644 2027 | DDC 781.64409--dc23

First Edition

Published in 2027 by
Gareth Stevens Publishing
2544 Clinton Street
Buffalo, NY 14224

Designer: Kathy Walsh/Beeline Media & Design, Inc.
Editor: Tricia Hoffman

Photo credits: Cover, SeventyFour/Shutterstock.com; cover, pp. 1–24 (music note background) Gaianami Design/Shutterstock.com; p 4 Anton Vierietin/Shutterstock.com; p 6 MIA Studio/Shutterstock.com; p 7 Master1305, Gorodenkoff/Shutterstock.com; p 8 Drazen Zigic/Shutterstock.com; p 9 @Wiki/Wiki; p 9 LaInspiratriz/Shutterstock.com; p 10 @Wiki/Wiki; p 11 Joseph Sohm/Shutterstock.com; p 12 L Paul Mann/Shutterstock.com; p 13 Kobby Dagan, Fouadbz/Shutterstock.com; p 14 Adam McCullough/Shutterstock.com; p 15 Brian Friedman, arvzdix, Fouadbz/Shutterstock.com; p 16 Elizabeth Dover/Shutterstock.com; p 17 Everett Collection/Shutterstock.com; p 18 Anton Vierietin/Shutterstock.com; p 19 Paul Vinten/Shutterstock.com; p 20 Ben Houdijk/Shutterstock.com; p 21 Moch. Dika As Sujud/Shutterstock.com; p 22 @Wiki/Wiki; p 23 Lucian Nuta/Shutterstock.com; p 24 PrinceofLove/Shutterstock.com; p 25 XanderSt, Ben Houdijk/Shutterstock.com; p 26 Ben Houdijk/Shutterstock.com; p 28 Arthur D'Amario III, mark reinstein/Shutterstock.com; p 29 lev radin, Everett Collection, Featureflash Photo Agency, Northfoto/Shutterstock.com

Printed in China

CPSIA compliance information: Batch #QS27GS: For further information contact Gareth Stevens, New York, New York at 1-800-542-2595.

Table of Contents

Rhythm and Blues

Close your eyes. Feel that beat? Your feet start tapping. Your head starts bobbing. You feel the music with your whole body. That's the magic of R&B music!

R&B stands for "**rhythm** and blues." When you listen to R&B, you'll hear singers with powerful voices. The music might be slow and sweet. Or it might be fast and funky. Either way, R&B music can touch your soul.

R&B is one of the most important types of music ever created. Let's dive into the world of R&B!

The Birth of R&B Music

R&B music was born in Black American communities in the 1940s. People mixed different types of music to create something brand new.

In the early 1900s, Black Americans were making blues and jazz music. Blues music was often slow and sad. It told stories about hard times. Jazz music was more upbeat. The catchy tunes made people want to dance.

Black American musicians also sang **gospel** music in churches. Singers would clap their hands. They would stomp their feet. Their voices would soar high and dip low. Gospel music was full of emotion and soul.

In the 1940s, musicians started mixing blues, jazz, and gospel together. They added electric guitars and new instruments. This exciting new music was called "rhythm and blues," or R&B for short.

R&B music became very popular. People would go to clubs and dance halls to hear live bands. The music made them feel good. It brought communities together.

Soon, people across America were falling in love with R&B. R&B music gave Black Americans a powerful voice.

Jerry Wexler

THE NAME GAME

The name *R&B* was created in 1948 by a music reporter named Jerry Wexler.

R&B Music Throughout the Years

R&B music kept changing and growing. In the 1950s and 1960s, R&B music helped create rock and roll.

Artists like Chuck Berry and Little Richard made fast, exciting music. Their music wasn't just R&B or rock and roll. It was a mix of both **genres**. They took the sounds of R&B and made it louder and faster. They paved the way for rock and roll.

Sam Cooke

At the same time, singers like Aretha Franklin and Sam Cooke sang with much emotion in their voices. People called them "soul singers." This led to a new type of R&B called soul music.

Aretha Franklin

THE QUEEN'S VOICE

Aretha Franklin could sing four octaves! That means she could sing super low notes and super high notes. She earned the nickname "Queen of Soul" when she was only 25 years old.

Motown came out of Detroit, Michigan, in the 1960s. This kind of music began as R&B. Then, it changed into its own special sound. Groups like The Supremes and The Temptations made catchy songs. Everyone wanted to sing along to them.

The 1970s brought funk music. This was R&B music with even more rhythm! Artists like James Brown and Earth, Wind & Fire made people get up and dance. Their music had strong **bass** lines that made it impossible to sit still.

Earth, Wind & Fire

Stevie Wonder

YOUNGEST STAR

Stevie Wonder is one of the most famous Motown artists ever. He was only 11 years old when he signed his first record deal! He has been blind since birth.

In the 1980s and 1990s, R&B music got smoother. Artists like Whitney Houston and Boyz II Men sang beautiful ballads. R&B also started mixing with hip hop music. Artists like Mary J. Blige created a new sound that combined singing with rap.

Beyoncé, Usher, and Alicia Keys became superstars in the 2000s. They used new technology to create amazing sounds. Their music mixes old and new styles in exciting ways.

Usher

Beyoncé

BEYONCÉ'S BIG BREAK

Before becoming a solo superstar, Beyoncé was in a girl group called Destiny's Child. The group, which was first called Girl's Tyme, formed in 1990. Beyoncé was only nine years old at the time!

Alicia Keys

What Makes Music "R&B"?

R&B singers are known for their amazing voices. They can sing high notes and low notes. They can sing softly or powerfully. Many R&B singers add **runs** and **riffs** to their singing. They quickly move up and down different notes. It is almost like their voice is dancing.

R&B music also has a strong rhythm section. It includes drums, bass guitar, and keyboards. These instruments create the beat that makes you want to move. In R&B, the rhythm is smooth and steady. It feels relaxed but exciting at the same time.

Mariah Carey

RECORD BREAKER

Mariah Carey holds the record for most number one songs by a solo artist—19! Her five-octave vocal range means she can hit notes most people can't even hear clearly.

R&B **lyrics** usually talk about feelings. Many R&B songs are about love. Other songs talk about personal struggles. Some talk about celebrations. R&B singers put emotion into every word.

R&B music makes people feel something deep inside. It has soul. It touches your heart. When you hear good R&B music, you don't just listen with your ears. You feel it in your whole body.

R&B Music Around the World

R&B music started in America. But it soon spread around the world. Musicians took the soul, rhythm, and emotion of R&B and added their own culture's flavor.

In the early 1960s, British groups like The Rolling Stones were influenced by the music they learned from American artists. Later, British artists like Adele and Sam Smith made their own R&B music.

Sam Smith

In Jamaica, R&B music mixed with local sounds. This helped create reggae music. Jamaican artists like Bob Marley took the rhythm and feeling of R&B and added island beats and styles.

Bob Marley

Japan has a huge R&B music scene. Japanese artists like Hikaru Utada make R&B songs in their own language. Many Japanese singers study American R&B. Then, they add their own special touch.

Hikaru Utada

Burna Boy

In Africa, R&B has mixed with traditional African music. Nigerian artists like Burna Boy and Wizkid mix R&B singing styles with African rhythms. This music is sometimes called Afrobeats. It is popular around the world.

R&B Music Today and Tomorrow

Today, songs by The Weeknd, Bruno Mars, and H.E.R. play on streaming services and radio stations. These artists perform at sold-out concerts. Their music videos get billions of views online.

Modern R&B sounds different from the R&B music of the past. But it still has that special soul and rhythm. Today's artists use computers, **synthesizers**, and recording software to make music in ways that weren't possible before. But they still focus on great singing and real emotion—just like the first R&B artists did 80 years ago.

SZA

R&B ON TIKTOK

Modern R&B songs often become hits on TikTok first. Artists like SZA and Steve Lacy have songs that went viral because millions of people made dance videos or lip-sync clips.

What will R&B music sound like in the future? Nobody knows for sure! R&B will keep changing. Young musicians will use new technology that hasn't even been invented yet.

R&B music has an amazing history. It started with people in Black American communities who had a story to tell. It grew into one of the most important and influential types of music ever. R&B has brought joy, comfort, and inspiration to billions of people around the world.

R&B Music Superstars

These R&B superstars are some of the most talented musicians ever. They've written incredible songs, won tons of awards, and performed for millions of fans around the world. Some of them started making music before your parents were even born, and some are making hits right now. But all of them have made their mark on the world of R&B!

Ray Charles
1950s-2000s

Ray Charles was called "The Genius." He is considered one of the most influential musicians ever. He mixed gospel, blues, and jazz to create R&B sounds. Even though he was blind, he played piano beautifully. He won 17 Grammy Awards during his long career.

Diana Ross
1960s-today

Diana Ross started as the lead singer of The Supremes. They were Motown's most successful girl group. She later became a solo superstar, movie star, and fashion icon. Her style and voice inspired millions of people. She's had hit songs in five different decades!

Prince
1970s-2010s

Prince wrote thousands of songs in his career. He mixed R&B with rock, funk, and pop to make his own special sound. He could play 27 different instruments! Prince wore sparkly purple clothes. He put on wild shows that made crowds go crazy.

Whitney Houston
1980s-2010s

Whitney Houston was called "The Voice." Her powerful singing gave people goosebumps. She sold more than 200 million records around the world. When Whitney sang the national anthem at the 1991 Super Bowl, some people said it was the best version ever!

Beyoncé
1990s-today

Beyoncé is one of the biggest superstars in the world. Her powerful voice and amazing stage shows inspire millions. She has won 32 Grammy Awards. That's more than any other artist ever! She writes her own songs and creates dances that fans all over the world learn.

The Weeknd
2010s-today

The Weeknd got his start by posting songs on YouTube that people loved. His voice is smooth and unique. His songs mix R&B with pop and electronic sounds. He's known for his cool red suit jacket that he wore while performing at the Super Bowl halftime show.

Glossary

ballads (BAL-uhdz): slow songs that usually tell a story, often about love

bass (base): the low, deep sounds in music that you can often feel in your chest

genres (ZHAHN-ruhz): types or kinds of music, like hip hop, rock, or pop

lyrics (LIR-iks): the words of a song that tell the story

rhythm (RITH-uhm): the repeated pattern of sound or movement in music, poetry, or dance

riffs (rifs): short, catchy musical phrases that repeat throughout a song

runs (ruhnz): when a singer quickly moves their voice up or down through a series of notes, usually in a smooth, flowing way

synthesizers (SIN-thuh-sye-zurz): electronic instruments that can create many different sounds using computers and technology